THE OPPORTUNITY
FOR RELIGION

THE OPPORTUNITY FOR RELIGION

IN THE
PRESENT WORLD SITUATION

BY
HARRY F. WARD

NEW YORK
THE WOMANS PRESS
1919

COPYRIGHT, 1919, BY
HARRY F. WARD

CONTENTS

CHAPTER	PAGE
I.	7
II.	21
III.	45
IV.	56

THE OPPORTUNITY FOR RELIGION

I

OF the much writing impelled by the Great War, that which deals directly with religion is a very small proportion. Of this, by far the greater part is concerned with the problem of personal faith and conduct, or with the effect of the war upon religion and the churches in the days to come. There is another phase of the subject that calls for consideration. What opportunity does the world crisis offer for religion to lead humanity into a better way of living? The answer to that question should point the path of duty for the religious individual, and upon the answer which the churches make to that inquiry their future will most certainly depend.

8 OPPORTUNITY FOR RELIGION

The war has developed the demand and opportunity for the reconstruction of society. Practically all the social forces are now massed in a mighty struggle to determine in what kind of a world and in what manner humanity shall live for a long time to come. Religion is one of these forces. How is it mobilized and to what end? Is there any spiritual imperative that religion can bring to bear upon the present world situation? Is it able to translate its ideals into collective conduct, to give content to the duties it has been teaching? These are the questions that demand an answer, for the final test of all religions is in the field of social action. By what they have to contribute to the welfare of humanity, is their ultimate worth to be determined.

Of course when we speak of religion, it is organized religion that is meant, and more particularly the leaders of organized religion. The term "church" is not adequate for our purpose. It needs to be remembered that

OPPORTUNITY FOR RELIGION

organized religion to-day comprehends not only the churches, but also a number of other agencies for religious instruction and propaganda. It needs still more to be remembered that in the modern world there are large religious forces, actual and potential, without the bounds of all organized religion, which can be mobilized and brought to bear upon the present situation by an adequate religious statesmanship. Such forces are particularly to be found in the world of labor.

The mind of the race is beginning to see what the heart of mankind has long felt — that there is no hope for humanity save in the working out of world-democracy, and world-democracy will never be developed unless a common religious dynamic operates among all peoples, of which humanity shall become increasingly conscious and to which it shall increasingly yield its allegiance.

A unique element in the present situation is the extent to which mankind is conscious that an hour of destiny has arrived. The fateful hours of the past were not known to many of those who lived in them. They were revealed afterward to the historian. But the people of to-day have eaten plentifully of the tree of knowledge. The laws of the physical universe, the history of the human race, the causes of social progress and decay — these are all an open book before this generation. The control of nature and of human society is now in the hands of the common people to an extent unimagined by even the leaders of the past. Not blindly as did men of other days do we take the road. We are not walking in darkness.

The knowledge of the possibilities that hang upon the outcome of this day is not merely the property of the wise men of the universities. All over the earth the plain people are taking the destiny of the race into their hands. This issue will not be decided by a few leaders gambling with the lives of the masses. The "silent masses" are

OPPORTUNITY FOR RELIGION

everywhere becoming articulate. The voice of the weaker and more backward peoples is heard. Their interests are now to be considered. The Orient takes its place beside the Occident. Japan and China enter into the family of nations with power. The common people of India get unto themselves self-government. Never before have so many peoples been consciously joined together in the choosing of their future. It is indeed mankind deciding its destiny.

Yet it is still true that in every land large numbers of people are not conscious of the issue of the hour and many more are only partially enlightened concerning it. These are often the so-called "better class" of people. In this fact lies one opportunity and duty for religion. As it makes a man conscious of his moral choices, so must it make the nations conscious of the results that will follow their decision. Its educational and preaching processes can be used to that end. There is a penalty in store for the priests who let the people perish for lack of knowledge, who suffer them to be led as sheep to the slaughter, by their own ignorance and prejudice, the wiles of selfish leaders, and the influence of a designing press. The fact that the people have the power to decide is no guarantee that they will make a deliberate decision. Professor George A. Coe has pointed out the difference between the action of a crowd and of a deliberative group. It is the duty of religion to develop the people into a deliberative group, that they may decide their own fate and the fate of the future intelligently, with a full knowledge of the whole situation and of all the issues involved in it.

The people must be brought to see life whole. At present they see it only partially, and usually from the standpoint of self-interest. One of the tragedies of the hour is that those who seek human welfare honestly, see only one side of it. This blinding of vision by self-interest has determined the

OPPORTUNITY FOR RELIGION

policy of religious and labor groups which were pledged to seek the good of all humanity. How much has their action been determined or will it be determined by some secret, half-recognized hope of advantage to themselves? How much is their point of view determined by the environment and training of their class interests? Religion should help men to rise above such narrow ground. It should give them knowledge of the whole situation and lead them to consider the interest of all. If the world is left in this hour of emergency to depend upon self-interest, it will be left to the mercy of an unreliable guide, for self-interest generally leads only to the satisfaction of immediate needs and desires. It is always difficult to see the larger and longer self-interest of following the ideal, to perceive the good that comes to one's self by seeking the good of others. Yet to get men and nations to seek this larger self-interest, to act for the good of the whole, is one of the special functions of religion.

If mankind is to make an intelligent choice in this situation, it must not only know the consequences of its decision, it must not only have in mind the interests of the whole of humanity; it must also see clearly the nature of the choice that is before it. It must know just what it is choosing. The question now before the house of humanity is the prevention of war. But behind war is the philosophy of the state that needs militarism for its support, and behind that is the social system out of which war emerges.

The ultimate fact behind the recent world-conflict is that the work life of the world is organized around the spirit of greed and conquest. No stable and enduring peace can be created without reckoning with this fact. If mankind would save itself from wasting death by a continued series of conflicts, it must find a new manner of living in times of peace. It is a choice not simply between two principles of government, but between two philosophies of life. The world must choose between life organized around the principle of strife, and life organized around the principle of good will. The way out of war and its horrors is not by paper pacts merely, but by the creation of a new world. It is not merely a question of new political constitutions or of new forms of social organization; it is also a question of motives and organizing principle. Shall civilization seek property or life, the creation of goods or the development of humanity? Shall its organizing principle be strife or love, service or exploitation, the right of the strong, as individuals and a class, to rule, or the duty of the strong to serve?

The choice now is between the religion of war and the religion of peace. The religion of war is glorious. It calls out all the energies of life in supreme moments of conflict. But it hurts and destroys. It is the religion of aristocracy. It makes supermen, who live in palaces. And they have many servants all over the earth, who do not live in palaces.

The religion of love is more glorious. It also requires courage, endurance, sacrifice. It calls out all the energies of life in a continuous conflict with nature and with evil, in a sustained career of service. It does not hurt or destroy, it heals and renews. It is the religion of democracy. It makes not lords but freemen, who choose to be "suffering servants" and who live not in palaces, but in carpenter shops. It develops a society of producers cooperating together in the production of economic goods and using them for the development of all the higher values of life, not for a chosen few, but for all the people.

The tendency of our times is to be content with the mere mechanics of change. Is religion at fault? Then let us see what is the matter with the churches. Let us get federation instead of competition; but that federation, having the same inadequate forms of religious expression, brings yet no new note into the spiritual life. In a day when

OPPORTUNITY FOR RELIGION

the present world-order is proving inadequate for both the practical needs and the spiritual desires of man, those of us who are Christians may well remember that weighty word of Chesterton that "the characteristic demand of Christianity is for a new world." To make that new world, religion must now challenge mankind. But if there is to be a new world, then religion, too, must have new forms of expression.

The need for a new world is a challenge to the will of man, and religion always makes its central appeal to the will. Religious workers in our training camps remarked upon the fact that the outstanding characteristic of the majority of the men was the lack of any definite or conscious purpose. They were living, and apparently were going to fight, without any aim. This fact is a revelation of the nature of our industrial civilization. Its largest conscious motive being the mere production of goods, it leaves the mass of mankind with nothing to do and no motive in life but to make or earn money and then to spend it. It is the business of religion to give life an aim, to fasten its eyes upon a high goal, and then to develop the will to hold the lagging feet in the path that leads thither. In a time when the nations who sit in darkness are seeking for light, when the peoples of the earth are treading together the wine-press of sorrow and suffering and cannot see the way out, it should be the distinction of religion to call the world to a great purpose.

One of the perils of the hour is that religious leaders should uncritically assume that such democratic gains have already come out of the war, that it will inevitably become a great instrument of social progress. But whatever gains have been achieved in the national control of industry, and in the increase of collective action, can easily be used for the strengthening of militarism. Or they can become the tools of a people seeking nothing higher than the increase of

OPPORTUNITY FOR RELIGION

material goods. The social gains of war time have yet to become the possessions of all the people, to be dedicated to the spiritual advancement of the whole race.

To make the choice that will lift humanity to new heights of living requires a great effort of the collective will. Before a new world can be organized mankind must passionately long for it, must definitely set its will to achieve it. Our later philosophers have pointed out that mankind, having the intellectual and mechanical tools of progress, yet lacks the desire and the will to create a better way of living. It is the business of religion in this day of opportunity to develop and guide the creative will of mankind to the shaping of a better form of society.

One of the deepest spiritual facts of the present hour is the growing apprehension of a new world-order. It seems almost within our grasp, yet somehow eludes our eager outstretched hands. It is the hour of travail for mankind. A new world is struggling to come forth and the old order is holding it back. It is an hour of torturing uncertainty, but the hour of a great hope. Everywhere is the portent of new things, the universal expectation of a great emancipation that has ever marked the beginning of a religious era.

The spirit of creation broods again, this time above the chaos of human relations. In the social unrest of the last generation and now in this world-conflict, there is more than a human struggle. The eternal Power is striving in and with us to bring order out of the anarchy of our political and economic affairs, to accomplish the divine dream of unity in this most difficult of all spheres. In this great hour can religion bring together the will of man and the will of God in a common creative effort? Is it possible to experience a collective incarnation?

II

It is significant that almost every one who writes about religion in the present situation laments sectarian divisions and desires more unity. This is a reflection of the world-effort toward a larger degree of united action. It is of a piece with the movement toward political federation and international control. The movement for religious coöperation contains the possibilities of a much larger service from religion to humanity, but it must face the question of the purpose and end for which the churches are to be federated or unified, it must recognize that present forms of religious expression have failed to satisfy so many of those who seek truth at one end of society and of those who struggle for social justice at the other end. Religion must reckon with the fact that the awakening working class in all the industrial nations has weighed our present civilization in the balance and found it wanting. They have condemned it not simply because it has failed to provide them with the necessary goods for the development of life, after they have labored to the utmost of their energy, but because it has thwarted their sense of justice, and denied them the satisfaction of their longing after brotherhood. They have condemned it then on moral and spiritual grounds. They are bent upon the making of a new civilization. They will have no use for any kind of religion which does not lead them in that endeavor, which condones or sustains the present order. If religion is to have any leadership in the future, if it is to meet the heart-hunger of the masses, it must show them a new manner of life.

In such an undertaking, the search for unity in religion must go farther afield. From the achievement of religious cooperation, it must proceed to develop cooperative religion. It must discover the common ele-

OPPORTUNITY FOR RELIGION

ment in all religions. It must emphasize those universal aspirations and ideals which will stimulate the joint undertaking for a better world. It must provide the atmosphere in which world-democracy can grow. There is need not only to mass the common spiritual resources of mankind but also to develop them to their maximum capacity. As the fierce test of war has demanded all the noble qualities of man, so the task of reconstruction, the necessity of creating a new world-order, will require all the spiritual capacities of the race. To raise such capacities to their highest possible power at this present moment is the contribution to the common undertaking demanded of religion.

The essential elements of religion were stated long ago in classic form: "Now abideth faith, hope, love, these three; and the greatest of these is love." What demands, then, does the adventure that now lies before mankind make upon these, its fundamental spiritual resources?

Mankind lives by faith. No step forward in life, individual or collective, is ever taken without it. The will to believe is also the will to create. The faith that cries, "It shall be done," actually removes mountains, achieves the impossible. Such faith is the indispensable condition of progress, because it leads men to attempt the unprecedented, to try the thing for which there is no proof, to dare the thing which never has been done. Donald Hankey found in the trenches that faith was "betting one's life that there is a God." This is exactly the quality that mankind needs for the task that lies before it. To achieve their need and their desire, the nations must risk their lives on the chance that the universe is with them, that the eternal order of things is justice and love. It is both the necessity and the desire of mankind to organize a world without arms, to organize industry within and between nations for the service of human need and not for the making of gain for the people of

OPPORTUNITY FOR RELIGION 25

power; and such a world has never yet existed. Already concrete plans to this end have been drafted. They are being soberly considered by responsible authorities, but it is something which never has been done and it will not be done without a great wave of faith throughout the world. The beginnings of a new order of life for mankind depend absolutely upon the generation of sufficient faith to make it possible to risk the first steps. It is always the peculiar duty of religion to develop the faith by which the work of the world gets accomplished. In such an emergency, when new reserves of faith are required, what a challenge comes then to religion!

Yet the war has struck heavy blows at faith. Facing the hard facts of conflict, the bitter evidence of the ambitions, the jealousies, the self-will of classes and nations, how many among us have less faith in humanity than before the war? How many of those who, when the war broke out, said

26 OPPORTUNITY FOR RELIGION

confidently, "This will be the last," are now saying, "Wars must always be," are urging their nation to prepare for the continuance of war, are assuming the present order of things as eternal, are repeating the vapid fallacy that "human nature cannot be changed," are evidencing a belief in the total depravity of mankind which they would indignantly reject if it were asserted concerning their own individual natures? How many have less confidence that the nations of the earth are amenable to reason and good will than they had before they encountered the hard reality of war? Yet the construction of an international and supra-national organization that shall order a new way of living for the world must be based upon mutual trust and good will. It requires more faith between men than there was before the war began and very much more than now exists.

This does not mean faith in a fool's paradise or faith in a kind of humanity which

OPPORTUNITY FOR RELIGION

does not yet exist, but to retain sanity and clarity of judgment there must be faith in the ultimate possibilities of mankind, in the potential goodness even of enemies. It is because we have not faith in each other and therefore have not faith in God that we continue armaments and competitive industrialism.

When religion addresses itself to the task of generating a faith adequate for the reconstruction of the world, it will face a widespread indifference. One of the inevitable consequences of the tremendous drain upon the energies of life by the recent struggle is the exhaustion of idealism. The forces of religion will have all that they can do to prevent a dull and deadly period of materialism, such as followed our own Civil War. The only hope is that they should now proceed to develop the unrealized spiritual reserves of those who are not exhausted by the actual conflict.

Many of the men who went to the front

found their better selves. They developed unrealized capacities. They know now what they can do in the face of death and the impossible. How shall the men who stayed at home be made to believe also in their better selves and in the possibilities of humanity? As the men in the trenches have come to feel the pull of comradeship and to know the crowd urge that calls faint-hearted men over the top to die gloriously, so must the people who have never felt the terrible uplifting enthusiasm of battle be led to act together upon their faith, until they also have discovered the powers that are within them and can apply to the making of a new world the same unrealized resources of idealism which have developed the heroism of the battle-field. Theirs it is to live to create the new world for which other men have died. For this more sustained endeavor they will need even a greater faith than that which inspires men deliberately to hazard their lives for an ideal.

OPPORTUNITY FOR RELIGION 29

Jesus lived and died by a faith in the ultimate supremacy of spiritual forces. He risked his life on the hypothesis that they would prove stronger than all the mailed might of the Roman Empire. In what does the majority of mankind trust to-day? In the power of the spiritual forces of love and service or in the power of hard facts, of money and munitions? It is a question of relative values. In which will we trust as the controlling forces in the organization of life?

Religion is challenged to make mankind to-day believe in itself and in God as it never has done before in its history. Otherwise its faltering feet may turn down the path that leads to destruction. If religion folds its hands and preaches the counsel of despair, if it does but echo the voice of the marketplace, crying that the ideals of humanity and the laws of God are both unrealizable, then indeed has the day of death begun to dawn for the peoples of the earth. The supreme

30 OPPORTUNITY FOR RELIGION

tragedy of a community or a nation is when its religion is merely the defender of the existing order, when the only God that the people are called to worship is the "God of things as they are." Life moves forward only when religion proclaims the things that ought to be and challenges the will of the people to make them be. If the collective will of mankind is now to be directed to the making of a new world, all the teaching agencies of religion must continually proclaim the vision of "a new heaven and a new earth." If now this should be made concrete in terms of disarmament and world-wide economic cooperation, the nations would soon come to believe these measures possible. If the people can be made to see, they will rise and follow the vision.

To make faith effective there must be added to it — hope. Hope brings faith down to the ground. It possesses insistency and immediacy. It looks to the near accomplishment of that which faith leads the will to

OPPORTUNITY FOR RELIGION

attempt. It believes not simply that the Kingdom of God will come sometime and somewhere, but that it will come even upon the earth as in heaven and that its beginning will be now. It believes that a different social order is not only possible, but is within reach.

Loss of hope is one of the inevitable accompaniments of war, for hope belongs with the vitality of youth, and the world is now war-weary and old. An American student at the French front commented upon the fact that the French soldiers are prematurely aged. "They have lost their youth," he says; "they sit like old men and talk constantly of the good days they have seen in the past." The world faces the task of reconstruction with much of its youth gone and with much that remains prematurely exhausted and aged. It is a less hopeful world; will it be a less moral, a less idealistic world? If our civilization is not to become prematurely impotent, the springs of youth and hope must be restored. To those of middle age and past, Bertrand Russell brings a great word concerning "the young men who have died through our fear of life. . . . Their very ghosts have more life than we. . . . Out of their ghosts must come life and it is we whom they must vivify." The generation now coming to manhood must be given more than the natural hope of youth. "It is necessary to create a new hope; . . . only a supreme fire of thought and spirit can save future generations from the death that has befallen the generation we knew and loved." [1]

One of the outstanding qualities of the Christian religion is its perennial youthfulness and hope. It refuses to despair before the entrenchments of evil, no matter how strong they be. It shouts its triumph in the very face of death. Christianity has a social gospel, and the social gospel refuses to acquiesce in the triumph of evil upon the

[1] Russell, "Why Men Fight."

OPPORTUNITY FOR RELIGION 33

earth; it believes that humanity can and will go on to perfection; it insists that the ideals and principles of Jesus which express and identify the ideals and aspirations of humanity and the eternal purposes of God shall yet be embodied in human living.

One of the continually recurring tendencies of religion is to transfer its faith to the hereafter. When evil has seized control of this present world, then the people of religion look for some future deliverance. So Israel, when great heathen powers were grinding her between their iron jaws, transferred her religious hope from the present to the hereafter. So the early Christians, suppressed by imperial Rome, looked away from the pomp and power of the scarlet woman upon the seven hills to the Christ coming from the clouds in glory to set up his reign upon the earth. The same tendency appears in this present time. In the presence of sin so vast, calamity so overwhelming, as this world-war, multitudes of Christians are taking refuge in the theory that the world is evil and must therefore either be destroyed or purged by the second coming of Christ to reign in power. As a demonstration of faith in the presence of world-catastrophe this is magnificent, but it is not religion. It abandons hope for the redemption of an evil world at the very time when the largest steps in the process of world-redemption are within reach, if only the faith and will of man can be joined with the eternal purpose and power of God.

The duty of religion in a time like this is plainly to increase the hope of mankind. This it can do by pointing out that the present situation is neither fate nor destiny, but the consequence of the ignorance and selfishness of man, the result of the teaching of false ideals and the organization of life on a wrong basis. Religious teaching can point out the responsibility for this and all other wars by analyzing their causes. It can encourage humanity to hope for the abolition

OPPORTUNITY FOR RELIGION 35

of war by showing the degree of control over the spirit of aggression which man has acquired through long years of social advance. It can point out how in former times individual men continually faced each other in arms and suspicion as the nations now do. It can show the progress that the nations have made in arranging peaceful methods to settle their disputes. It can show the development that has been made since the war began in the joint control of the economic causes of war. It can point out the spread of the desire and determination to make an end of this common enemy of the race. Lest mankind should now stop short of this desired goal and even of its possible achievement in the present situation, there must be a concerted effort to strengthen the hope of men.

There remains "the greatest of these — love." Without love, faith may not realize its vision nor hope its purpose. It is not only "the greatest thing in the world," but the greatest need of mankind in this crisis. Jesus revealed a God of love. A new commandment He gave men, that they should love one another. This was to be the sign of God-likeness and in the doing of it they were to find fellowship with God. He proclaimed love as the welding force of the community life that was to develop around his teaching. He taught love as the organizing principle of human fellowship. His disciples were to concrete it in service to one another, and this was to distinguish them from the Gentiles. His followers have long proclaimed love as the greatest personal virtue. They have striven to be made perfect in love. It is now time for them to proclaim and develop love as the only social force sufficient to bind humanity together in the new world-life that its faith and hope are seeking. In this effort they will be joined by a great company, for good will is the talisman of all modern idealists — the force in which they put their trust.

OPPORTUNITY FOR RELIGION 37

The innate capacity of mankind to love and the extent to which the passion for brotherhood has gripped the heart of mankind have been amply shown by the war. It was a hard war to make. So far had good will between the nations developed that among the common people the will to hate and to kill had to be cultivated by invented acts of aggression, by exhortations of preachers and would-be poets, by the sight and recital of atrocities and by training in ferocity. This manifest reluctance to make war is not because the battle spirit of man has atrophied in an industrial civilization. The unsurpassed endurance and heroism in the trenches of men who until recently had never thought of war as a possibility is evidence enough to support the contention of those who maintain that the struggle of civilization to subdue both nature and the barbaric instincts of mankind will retain all the virtues that lie in the battle spirit of the race. It is difficult to make war to-day because the ancient dream of shepherds and the Holy Grail of the wise — good will among men — has become a modern social fact of the first importance. Alongside the latent barbarism brought to the surface by this war must be chronicled a desperate effort to maintain good will, to hold on to the spiritual gains acquired in the slow ascent of man.

Yet the common stock of good will that is the great social inheritance of mankind has been sadly impaired by the recent struggle. The natural recuperation of the spirit of good will among the fighting men after the battle is over is one of the marvels of history, even as the recuperative power of the physical organism when wounded is one of the marvels of nature. But something more will be needed for reconstruction days than natural good will. There will be needed greater cooperative capacity, which is more than the ability to fraternize or to worship together. These forms of association provide no guarantee against the repetition of

OPPORTUNITY FOR RELIGION 39

the present horror, for men have joined in these and still have been dragged unwillingly into war to kill each other. What is needed to make good will effective in social cooperation is a definite discipline, both of teaching and of practice, and this it is the function of religion to develop.

Effective good will is the development of the social process, as well as of the proclamation of an ideal. It can therefore no more be conjured out of the air for the great task of reconstruction than can the metal that has been shot into the soil of Europe or the lumber that has been splintered in the trenches. There is a long-continuing process of creation behind the one as the other. To repair the breaches the war has made in international good will is a task as difficult as knitting together the broken economic life of the world. Indeed, the two undertakings are interdependent. In this task of reconstruction it is time to add to our regimen of conservation of economic materials a similar effort to conserve our spiritual resources. Unless the world can do this, it will find itself spiritually bankrupt, in its day of greatest opportunity.

The loftiest expression of good will is the command of Jesus, "Love your enemies." This teaching is the climax of the endeavor of mankind to establish brotherhood, the culmination of a slow development of ethical standards. Only through long periods of social advance did men learn that distrust and hostility toward the stranger without the gates was not essential to loyalty to their own group. Slowly did they discover that the wider the extension of mutual aid, the greater its benefits to all concerned. Finally they sought after world-wide brotherhood. But this goal cannot be attained without the ability to deal in good will with those who are aggressors against the common weal.

This cannot be done by assuming or refusing to assume certain personal relationships to other persons. It is a question of

OPPORTUNITY FOR RELIGION 41

the relations between nations and groups of nations. To find out how to love one's enemies becomes a matter of discovering a policy for the nation that shall really embody good will as an active principle and leave no abiding enmity.

To develop good will between enemies, to eliminate the bitterness and hate of war time, the essential thing is a common purpose, a policy and program of common action. Religion approaches this undertaking with the advantage that it already has under its direction people who had a common purpose before the war. One of the great spiritual tragedies of the war was that it caused the "brothers" and "comrades" of a chosen fellowship to seek each others' lives. They had and still have a common religious purpose, but another interest separated them from their common purpose and from each other. It was the need and demand of the state that did this. If this need and demand does not coincide with the larger good of all mankind, to seek which religion has been calling into a common fellowship the citizens of different states, then the state has achieved a stronger moral sovereignty than religion, and religion stands defeated. In such case, the first task of religion is to recall its own adherents to the common fellowship by rekindling their loyalty to their common purpose. If it cannot do this, how can it ever teach the rest of the world to "love your enemies"?

Ought not adherents of the same religion in hostile countries to inquire whether they have a common interest which is higher than the interest that separates them? If their religion has taught them that God must be expressed in a world-wide life of brotherhood, must they not continually inquire how much their national aim is making for this larger good, and thus find out how national pride and self-interest are obstructing the vision of God? If these religious groups would thus seek together after their com-

OPPORTUNITY FOR RELIGION

mon purpose, would they not find a common way for their nations out of their antagonism, and thereby develop a common force for reconstruction? The hope of advance for mankind depends upon whether the forces of good will possess the capacity to organize their common passion for brotherhood, to develop into conscious fraternity the "mutual aid" which has been the principal factor in social evolution, and to direct it to the chosen end of a world-wide, cooperative life.

This means that religion must call its adherents in every land to a passionate loyalty to its ideal of world-wide brotherhood. In war time the state achieves national solidarity and safety by calling individuals to a sacrificial loyalty. The achievement of the solidarity of mankind requires the continuous expression of loyalty, to the point of sacrifice. Herein is accomplished the supreme religious expression of the individual. To secure this abundant life of sacrificial loyalty to the greatest possible cause is the compelling duty of religion. It must ever call the peoples of the earth to follow at any cost the way of love, which is the only way of life.

III

RELIGION has also a duty other than developing the spiritual resources of mankind. It must lead them to expression. It is faced with the necessity of deciding what policies of national and international action will realize its faith, embody its hope, and give concrete expression to its love. In this hour of choice, when humanity stands in the valley of decision, religion must express itself concerning the next steps for humanity to take in the direction of the ideals which it has been proclaiming. It must teach mankind not simply duty, but the content of duty.

The approach to this concrete expression of religion is always twofold. It involves both measures of repression against evil and constructive measures to replace evil with good. If a community is to get rid of the curse of alcohol, there must be both the elimination of the organized saloon and the development of constructive social recreation to take the place of the fellowship that has ever gathered around the drink habit. So will it be in the world situation. The making of a better world involves the destruction of giant evils. In order to transfer the heroic religious qualities of war time to the slower and quieter task of social reconstruction, that task must be shown to involve conflict. It must involve the supreme thrill of the shock of battle. An enemy makes men heroes. The necessity of resisting idolatry, slavery, the liquor traffic, has glorified very ordinary people. One of the duties of religion is to identify and reveal the forces of evil, in order that mankind may know against what its toil and heroism should really be directed.

The spirit of antagonism has a social value. Animated by self-interest, it drives

OPPORTUNITY FOR RELIGION

men against each other. Concentrated upon a common foe, it binds men together. In the presence of a common enemy, there develops at once loyalty to a common cause and capacity for common action. The world of labor is continually divided by internecine conflicts. There are jurisdictional strikes between different trade unions. There is perpetual conflict between the socialist, the trade-unionist, and the syndicalist. Let some dull-minded and overgreedy capitalist, however, launch an assault upon one of the fundamental rights and liberties of labor and at once they are united against the common menace. How many years of development in the ordinary constructive processes of peace would it have taken to get the Allied Powers to cooperate, as they did under the pressure of a common foe, in the joint administration of their economic life? Could the nations but come to see that poverty is their common menace, and that greed is destroying them all alike, they would extend this joint administration until the whole world would be bound together in a common cooperative life.

The two great forces that mankind together must conquer are nature and evil. The one, man must conquer for the means of subsistence, the other for his spiritual development. In the present circumstance, the evil that is in the world and in man has been dramatically personified in war. War is the common enemy.

The physical horrors of war are the lesser of its evils. It is the effect of war upon the souls of men and the soul of the world-organism that must be faced. In considering what war does to personality, it must be remembered that personality is a social fact. The most serious consequence of war is its assault upon the growing social personality of mankind, in which alone our individual personalities come to their full realization. In the present state of the world-life, war is indeed fratricidal — not simply because it

OPPORTUNITY FOR RELIGION 49

requires brothers and comrades, pledged to a common cause, to kill each other, but because it turns one part of the social body against the other part. It is the dread disease, the terrible madness that causes mankind to devour its own vitals.

There are two groups of proposals before the common parliament of humanity, looking toward the abolition of war and the establishment of world-order. One comes from intellectuals, who are now managing the affairs of the world. They are planning a League of Nations to adjust the disputes of the world and thus to develop a stable and enduring peace. Some of them make disarmament an essential feature of the plan, but more do not. The other proposal comes from the men who labor with their hands. They are demanding that the nations shall be disarmed and that the economic life of the world shall be reorganized on the basis of cooperation instead of competition, that it shall be developed in friendship and mutual

50 OPPORTUNITY FOR RELIGION

aid instead of in strife and war. In these proposals there are two great central facts around which the mind and purpose of humanity needs now to concentrate: disarmament and economic cooperation. The first steps in these two processes must now be taken if the world is to learn to walk in a new way of life. It is for or against these things that the nations must now choose.

Religion has long proclaimed a day when the sword should be beaten into the plowshare and the spear into the pruning-hook. That day is within reach. Weary of slaughter, fearful of its disastrous economic consequences, conscious of the burden of armaments upon the productive energies of humanity, the peoples of the earth are looking for a way of disarmament. When the first universal measure is taken to that end, the death warrant of war is sealed. War is collective crime, and armaments are its tools and occasion. They do not make war, but they provide the means for war and they

OPPORTUNITY FOR RELIGION

make it inevitable. An ex-premier of Great Britain feels it necessary to appeal to us not to repeat the fallacy they have at such cost disproved — that armaments make for peace. The English Council of Workers and Soldiers says: "If the nations are not loaded, they cannot explode." Wilfully to continue armaments is to continue the occasion and incitement to international crime. It is as if the drunkard had power to abolish the saloon and willed to continue it. Yet there are those who are now working for the continuance of armaments; some from the motive of profit, others from fear, others from a limited and misguided patriotism. Assuming the permanence of war, they are doing their best to make its continuance inevitable by working for policies which will increase the distrust and suspicion of mankind. At a time when faith needs to be aroused for the great adventure of a warless world they are spreading the deadly narcotic of disbelief. In a day when it is possible for mankind to throw off its back the burden of militarism they are transmitting paralysis of the will. In this day of supreme opportunity they are revealing themselves as traitors to the commonwealth of man.

If the world does not get disarmament, the sacrifices of this conflict will have been in vain. Men said the Napoleonic wars were to be the last of war. It was an idle dream. It always will be until the will and purpose of mankind is united to achieve disarmament. This is now a possible accomplishment. Unless it be done, mankind will be enslaved to the economic burden of this war. Neither the forces of labor, of intellect, nor of religion can do their full work for the world if they must carry this handicap in the future. President Wilson has made a measure of disarmament one of his war aims. In timid, hesitating fashion some of the statesmen of Europe have partially echoed his words. "We hope," says one, "that disarmament will be included in

OPPORTUNITY FOR RELIGION

the terms of peace." And while they hope they fear. Just before his death, at the front, viewing the possibility that the war may be settled on the basis of trade, leaving economic competition between the nations, Professor T. F. Kettle wrote: "It will be a victory tainted with ambiguous and selfish ends. History will write of us that we began nobly but that our purpose corrupted. The great war for freedom will not indeed have been waged in vain, that is already decided, but it will but half have kept its promises. Blood and iron will have been once more established as the veritable masters of men and nothing will open before the world but a vista of new wars."[1] The one sure prevention of this disaster is to secure disarmament. Has the United States, the youthful nation, the faith, the courage, the initiative to lead the old world in this enterprise? What leadership has its religion to offer in this emergency?

[1] Kettle, "The Ways of War."

54 OPPORTUNITY FOR RELIGION

To achieve disarmament is a constructive task. It demands new methods of political organization, new forms of dealing with international disorder. It is the task of statesmanship to work out the measures, it is the duty of religion to demand that the process shall now be commenced. It is the first general measure around which the international forces of religion can rally as the common shepherds of humanity. If all religious teaching the world over should constantly expound the necessity and the possibility of universal disarmament, if from every pulpit, in every Sunday-school, in every religious paper, this demand should be persistently reiterated, would not the world-will presently be aroused and made intelligent to achieve this great step in human progress? Disarmament is more than a mechanical measure. It leaves untouched the economic causes of war, the deep-rooted battle instinct which has to be given expression, but it clears the way for these under-

OPPORTUNITY FOR RELIGION

takings. It removes the incubus of fear and suspicion which makes love and cooperation impossible. It is the expression of a great spiritual purpose. It is the beginning of a new way of life. That step taken, the world would not long consent to continue its economic life on the basis of war; its impetus would send mankind on up to new heights of living. The removal of fear will lead to the extension of international relationships in every field, to the removal of all barriers opposing the free interchange of both economic goods and intellectual and spiritual gains, to the gradual cooperative control of all energies and resources for the fullest possible development of the whole of mankind. The idealism that has gone into a conflict of destruction will be turned into a competitive struggle of good will and service for the common good of humanity. Unknown capacities of production and cooperation, undreamed intellectual powers and spiritual resources, will be released.

IV

WHEN religion attempts the abolition of war, it will find that it must get back of the battle-field. War is a great school-master, and while religion has been busy dealing with things of the past, the facts of the present have been educating mankind. Many of the men who have seen reality in the trenches have gone back of the physical conflict to the organization of the spirit of the war in the daily life of man. They have come to know that we have a social system organized on the principle of conflict, within which the seeds of this death have been developing. They have come to see that what they endured in the trenches they have long suffered on the battle-fields of industry in times of peace — privation and pain, wounds and death. Now they are beginning to dis-

OPPORTUNITY FOR RELIGION

cover the cause of their suffering and to seek its removal. While the statesmen are talking of arbitration to settle disputes and a League of Nations to Enforce Peace, the working people are talking about the removal of the economic causes of war. In the blaze of a world conflagration they have come to see that back of war is the great fact that the everyday productive business of life is organized on the basis of strife; that it is a constant struggle between individuals, between groups, between nations, each seeking the rewards of victory in industrial plunder, in profit and education and luxury.

If religion is to lead the common assault of humanity against war, it must first understand the nature of war. Long ago Adam Smith, the great English economist, taught that war is largely due to the crimes of traders. A general of the United States Army said to a gathering of financiers, "You make the wars; we soldiers only end them." A recognized English authority on the Balkan situation insists that either of the two recent Balkan wars could have been prevented if the French bankers had been forbidden to finance the combatants![1] The same writer later said, regarding the overseas projects of financiers, "To my mind militarism is in the modern world the conception of life which thinks such adventure legitimate, and organizes for this. The worst of the German extremists wanted the Belgian coal fields and the French iron fields; ours happen to want the corn and cotton lands of Mesopotamia."[2]

Those who would destroy war must come to know that industrialism has been organized around the same principles and in the same form as militarism. It has massed large armies of workers under the control of absolute commanders who brook no challenge to their imperious will and suppress dissent by force. It has been accompanied by all the consequences of war. It has produced

[1] Brailsford, "The War of Steel and Gold."
[2] Brailsford, *The Herald*, London, May 9, 1917.

famine and pestilence. It has accomplished a vast destruction of life. Armies of cripples are flung off from its advance. It strengthens all the old causes of war, and constantly develops new occasions of conflict. It asserts the right of the strong to rule and makes the weak the prey, and the earth the booty, of the mighty. It develops economic imperialism in which the great nations compete for trade routes, undeveloped resources, the financial exploitation of weaker peoples. Its policy of "peaceful penetration" by foreign investment and commercial control is but another term for ruthless, aggressive ambition, is the brutal assertion of the will to power in the economic world, and is the constant provocation to strife. With its external expansion constantly leading in the direction of war, industrialism is also ever impelled in the same direction as a diversion and a means of control for the inevitable social unrest developed within the nation by its policies.[1]

[1] Veblen, "The Nature of Peace."

If there is to be a peaceful world, the spirit of war must be exorcised from economic life.

It lies within the province of religion to make the people understand that Mars is to-day a two-faced deity. Seen from the front by admiring worshipers he is a glorious figure in shining armor, clean and youthful, straight and compelling, with noble countenance; but on the other side, inseparably joined to this fair youth, is the gross and ugly figure of aged Mammon, with his feet upon the neck of prostrate womanhood, gripping little children by the throat with his fat hands. To destroy Mars, Mammon also must be overthrown. Here indeed is a warfare for religion. As Jesus said, "Ye cannot serve God and Mammon." As long as civilization is organized mainly to produce goods, it will continue in destructive strife. When it is organized to produce men and women, to develop the spiritual values of life, it will come to be a cooperation in mutual service.

OPPORTUNITY FOR RELIGION

Will religion accept the challenge of its mighty foe and lead humanity against the common enemy? There came a day when Jesus must needs turn aside from his preaching and teaching, and go to Jerusalem to join the final issue with the chief priests and Pharisees and with Pilate, knowing that the Cross was the end. There came a day when Paul must cease his missionary journeying, and go to Rome, "not knowing what shall befall me there," to join the issue with the imperial power of the Caesars. Has the day not come for modern religion at any cost to join the issue with the rulers of our civilization, to call the hosts of humanity to hurl Mars and Mammon from their throne, to rid the earth forever of the curse of militarism and capitalistic industrialism?

Mars and Mammon being inseparably joined, must be destroyed together. The beginning of disarmament is the death-wound of Mars. The beginning of economic cooperation is the death-blow of Mammon. A

League of Nations with no agreement concerning their economic needs would leave untouched the roots of future conflicts. Or disarmament may mean the joining of the great powers together in a compact of benevolent economic imperialism to exploit together the weaker peoples and divide the booty, with some measure of justice between the spoilers, with none for the despoiled. For them there would be only a little kindness and that only as long as they were docile.

The alternative to such a league of dishonor is a world-wide extension of the cooperative principle. The Federal Council of Churches of Christ in America has declared for "equal rights and complete justice for all men in all stations of life." This needs to be applied to the nations and races of the earth to the uttermost extent. The same body has also approved the report of its Social Service Commission declaring for "the fullest possible cooperative control of both industry

OPPORTUNITY FOR RELIGION 63

and the natural resources upon which industry depends." This principle needs also to be extended to the economic relations between nations.

If religion would sweep away an ancient evil, it must replace it with a newer good. If arms and the glory of war are to be abolished, humanity must be brought together in a constructive fellowship of adventure and heroism. There must be developed "the moral equivalent of war." The toil and suffering and fellowship of the battle must be replaced by the toil and suffering and fellowship of the struggle to meet the daily needs of the race. Here religion will find content for its duties and realization for its ideals. It will express itself in such practical questions of statesmanship as the internationalizing of trade routes and waterways, the joint control of the distribution of raw materials. A religion which seeks the spiritual unity of the race must recognize that it is in the business of economic pro-

64 OPPORTUNITY FOR RELIGION

duction and exchange that the greatest development of cooperative capacity has come to mankind. This has led to his cooperative intellectual and spiritual development. The expansion of economic cooperation will release still greater capacities for mutual advance. Those who seek to impose their way of life upon others by force destroy both themselves and others. Those who join together to share their mutual capacities for the common good enlarge both their own and the common life. The principle of the cooperative national and international control of industry has gone far enough and been successful enough in the present war to make practicable its further extension.

It is through the development of economic cooperation that the world-family will solidify itself, and the world-order will develop. A league of peace which deals only with political questions is but a paper pact. The workers of the world have gone beyond the intellectuals in that they propose to give the organized supra-nation some task at once to accomplish, and it is only by action that organisms develop. Moreover, in this they are in actual tune with the facts and needs of to-day, for the business of economic production has now proceeded far beyond the political organization of mankind. Politically we are living in one century and economically we are living in another. The artificial boundaries of the states do not correspond to the facts of economic production and exchange, any more than they correspond to the ideal of fellowship and the capacity for its enjoyment. There are to-day no independent economic units. These absolute sovereignties, called states, which exist in political philosophy and practice, do not exist when it comes to the interdependent, economic life of the world, which crosses all frontiers. Here is the actual beginning of that world-family life to which religion seeks to call the loyalty of the individual and of the nation. An organization to express the fact of this growing world-unity will find that its authority rests not in any external power, but in its service value to humanity. Just as the nation contributes to the larger life of the individual, so will this world-organization contribute to the larger development of the nations and to the fullest happiness and expansion of mankind. Is the pull of self-interest sufficient to draw mankind to its accomplishment? Or does it need the passion of a great ideal to pull the world up to this new order of living, even as the passion to preserve the Union was finally needed to accomplish the final overthrow of slavery? Will its coming wait for the continuous proclamation by religion of the ideal of world-unity as the very expression of God, until there is massed for its accomplishment all the heart-hunger for the Infinite, all the passion for brotherhood, which are but different aspects of "the incurably religious nature" of all mankind?

Date Due

Library Bureau Cat. no. 1137